The Sea Quells

Also by Amy Evans

Collecting Shells (Oystercatcher Press)
VierSome #01 (with Nat Raha, Rebecca Cremin
and Frances Kruk, Veer Books)

THE SHEARSMAN CHAPBOOK SERIES, 2013
Martin Anderson *The Lower Reaches*
Richard Berengarten *Imagems 1*
Susan Connolly *The Sun-Artist*
Amy Evans *The Sea Quells*
Alice Kavounas *Thin Ice*
Tin Ujević *Twelve Poems (translated by Richard Berengarten)*

The
Sea Quells

Amy Evans

Shearsman Books

First published in the United Kingdom in 2013 by
Shearsman Books
50 Westons Hill Drive
Emersons Green
Bristol
BS16 7DF

www.shearsman.com

ISBN 978-1-84861-314-0

Cover: 'Mixed Layer' by David Rees

The following sequence is a following sequence. Its poems are a transliteration and continuation of *Collecting Shells*.

quell |kwel|
verb [trans.]
put an end to (a rebellion or other disorder), typically by the use of
force: *extra police were called to quell the disturbance.*
- subdue or silence someone: *Lawrence quelled him with a
  look.*
- suppress (a feeling, esp. an unpleasant one): *Patricia spoke up
  again to quell any panic among the assembled youngsters.*
- pacify: *she quelled her fears.*
- overcome or allay: to quell pain; to quell grief.

ORIGIN Old English *cwellan* [kill,] of Germanic origin; related
to German *quälen* 'torture.'

Synonyms
calm, soothe, settle, quiet, allay, assuage, overcome;
literary – stay.

IN TRO(TH)

Read   (These)   Together

       to gather
a rime
       of an unancient,
       unmarryner
a rif/t
       to re-member
to nurse
       erry rhyme

while (not)
        out to get/her,
She gathers

under(the)taking

UNCOLLECTED [S] H ELLES

as if trying on lone somes

    relationship-shaped

a brittle bit of

    self-scape

ape

    [d]

in words :

    un read,

foss*ill*s

    begin to br*ai*lle,

touched

see sure . . .

(a)gain s

(night) watch : bubbles up

        on down body

in bath bathed

        without tide

when *tired* tried to

        its limits,

lathered

        p(o)ore

society, *tired*all:

                                            no longer

fresh or in good(s)

                                            condition.

esp. of statement or idea

                                            (not) *boring or un*

interesting because over

-familiar,
                       family the same
& alliterative litter
                       taking up time
as it tells. I still resist

the weeded *we[']d*
                       because not
— and of —
                       ova,
learning earnt
                       dis-earns

up, date

                   yet that centre
s[c]ent [≈]
                   home
still con
                   seeds
a bloom

a stint   of time & petall

a gone

from

not yet long(ing)

       ago(ne)

and me-blossom, a while

of s kin

d shade

hangs around,

the *in*

stirring to touch

places

*tim(e)*ate

of a live

as if *shell* can not stand
      [it]
on its own
      is not a[n f] word for
that which soft I
          could not live with
    out
being preyed ~~upon~~
       open

bullets all   (over) spent

incase s   all s hell

breaks   lo(o)se

(cl)ever huntress rubbed dry,
         (b)listered she,
                              forced [her self /
                                    pursued]
                         by *suit*or
          out of
          [comfort]
Oh   zone

ad*or*ers all out of *or*der but

re member t*hes*e :

m a k e l e s s

       s e n s e (*but are*) m o r e

and No, Shout(ing) simplifies
                         LOVE
and its c ravings,   H ATE,

an ap/petite 4   uncunning punning
                         leased of

ALL
:[spl]UTTER

This, my calmer accretion reg(u)arded,
             though splendours sped
to spend time on   (: page   )
             surface pressure d now un fathoms able
leagues under
             and only just
crawling
        first

after
        a home, sure,
a land
        -mine
to blow open the once upon
        the wrack
the un-scene Now
        seen, back
and back,
        for mer

for the mere *mère*,
                    from the child
-less : whore ded measures,
                    liquid
all concockted,
                    shantily clad   a   drift
~~of~~
in the matterial
                    , missing

Last Scene :

                Be For e

left

no   right

                            (to) t/axe

        my bed

(No)   -Room   F/or
        pre-emptive/ly   ar Rest.
        kettles unquiet,

need   (doesn't)   sleap
I Am:
        b[r]/ought   (to)
        b/oil

See creature:

('I's)   (eyes)

wet

AFTER WORDS

In truth, it is
             quite
an undertaking
             to (Be)
Quiet under the taking
             esp. when
             *so lo*ansum

sea-"she"lf lies
             there,
(What Is)   hard,

must suffice   surface
         to say
with(out)
             attracting
interest

*s*ea-s*hell*f encrusts,

she sells sea shelf   *for her crust*

sea-*shell*f enc rusts,
                              creates
surf/

face   see?—

shellf quells
                    to put an end   :   bo(u)nd   ed

'til next tied

www.ingramcontent.com/pod-product-compliance
Lightning Source LLC
Chambersburg PA
CBHW021947040426
42448CB00008B/1288